I0151572

ALEX AND THE HEN

Ann Marie Bell

Published by

TEACH Services, Inc.
PUBLISHING
www.TEACHServices.com • (800) 367-1844

Copyright © 2025 Ann Marie Bell
Copyright © 2025 TEACH Services, Inc.
Published in Calhoun, Georgia, USA
ISBN-13: 978-1-4796-1809-5 (Paperback)
ISBN-13: 978-1-4796-1810-1 (ePub)

Alex couldn't wait for his summer adventure to begin at Grandma's farm. As soon as his parents pulled into the driveway of the old farmhouse, the curious ten-year-old boy eagerly peered out the car window, ready to explore.

Grandma burst from her rocking chair on the veranda and greeted her beloved grandchildren with big hugs.

After a hearty farm lunch, Alex and his sister Meredith dashed outside, ready to see what new surprises awaited them.

In the barnyard, a gray donkey brayed a welcome and a white goat bleated hello. But it was Grandma's clucking chickens that always fascinated Alex the most, with their colorful feathers and the way they laid so many eggs.

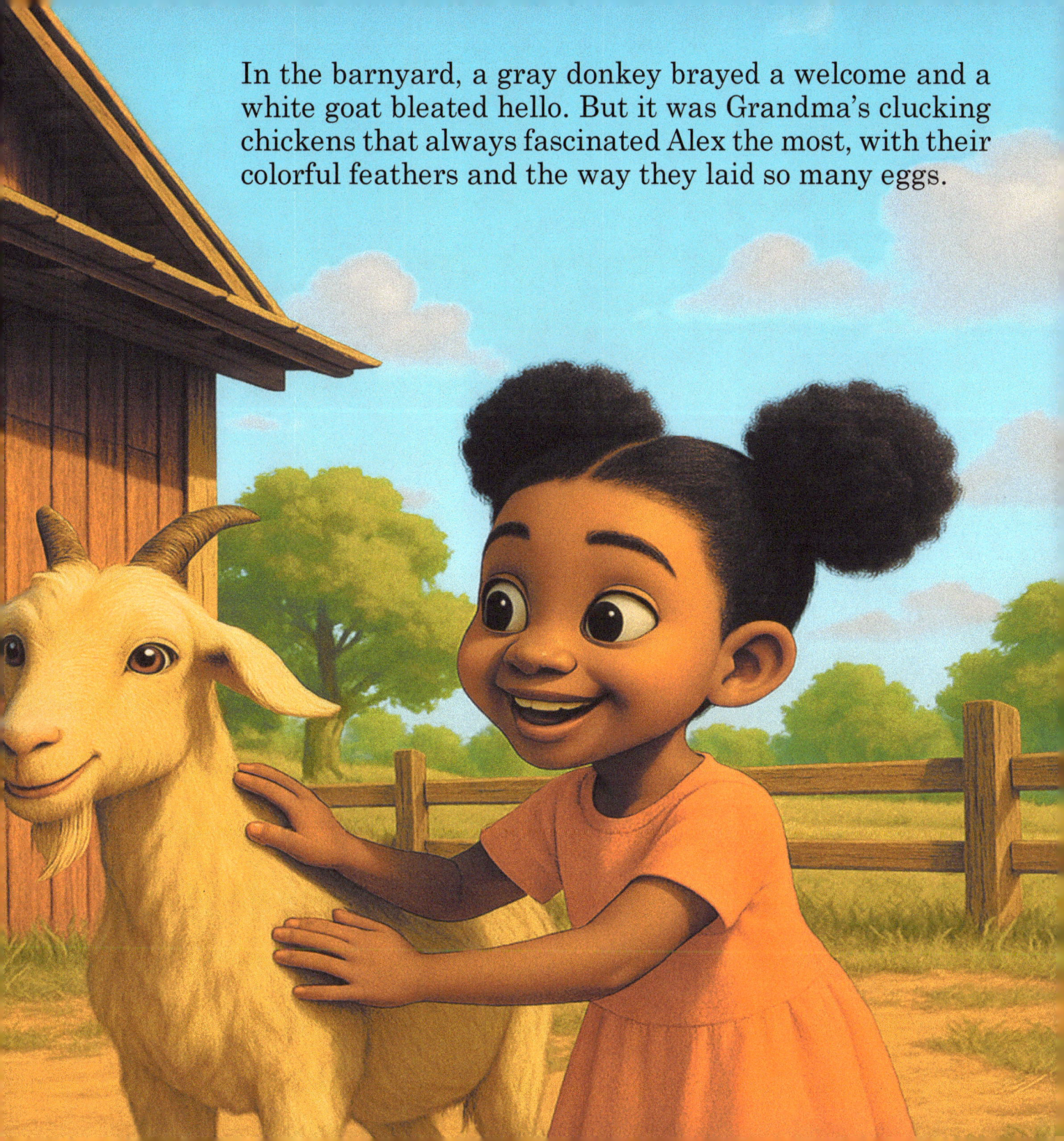

Alex hatched a plan—he would ask for a hen of his very own! But alas, Grandma needed all her hens for her farm business.

Still determined, the clever boy decided to buy a hen from the widow down the road. He would use the money he'd saved from his allowance.

At the widow's humble farm,
chickens pecked at food scraps.

She couldn't afford proper feed.

Alex's eyes lit up
as she agreed
to sell a hen.

He put the money in her hand and happily scooped up the hen of his choice. He couldn't wait to take his new feathered friend home!

In Grandma's chicken coop, Alex crafted the perfect nesting spot for his special hen, complete with store-bought feed and a water bowl.

He just knew she'd
be one happy hen,
laying egg after egg
in her comfy new
home.

But the next morning, Alex's hen was nowhere to be found!

He searched high and low, even calling "Coo-coo-coo!" until he was out of breath.

Finally, he found her back at the widow's farm, happily scratching for food as if she'd never left.

Alex couldn't believe it!
He scooped up the hen
and marched her right
back to her deluxe coop.

But the next day, she vanished again. She had scurried back to the widow's house.

The determined boy made several more attempts to get his hen to stay put, but she just kept fluttering back "home" to the widow.

Finally, Alex returned the hen and got his money back. He pondered the mystery as he trudged down the lane to Grandma's.

"Grandma, why did my hen always go back to the widow?" Alex asked.

Grandma smiled and explained, "She was used to the widow's call, so she followed her voice."

This made Alex think about all the voices people listen to in life.

"It's just like how Jesus wants us to follow Him," Grandma shared wisely.

"He wants to be our friend and give us good things to make us happy. The more we listen to His voice—by praying and reading the Bible—the more we will want to stick close to Him."

Alex nodded slowly. Even though he was young, he could start listening for Jesus' voice too. What an adventure that would be!

As Matthew 19:14 says, "Let the little children come to me ... for the kingdom of heaven belongs to such as these."

TEACH Services, Inc.
P U B L I S H I N G

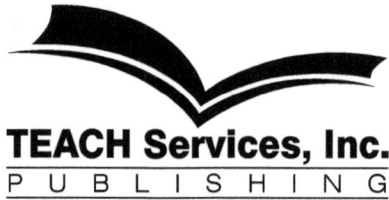

We invite you to view the complete
selection of titles we publish at:
www.TEACHServices.com

We encourage you to write us
with your thoughts about this,
or any other book we publish at:
info@TEACHServices.com

TEACH Services' titles may be purchased in
bulk quantities for educational, fund-raising,
business, or promotional use.
bulksales@TEACHServices.com

Finally, if you are interested in seeing
your own book in print, please contact us at:
publishing@TEACHServices.com

We are happy to review your manuscript at no charge.

www.ingramcontent.com/pod-product-compliance
Lightning Source LLC
Chambersburg PA
CBHW061416090426
42742CB00026B/3485